Life Cycles
From Caterpillar to Butterfly

First published in the UK in 2004 by
QED Publishing
A division of Quarto Publishing plc
The Fitzpatrick Building
188–194 York Way, London N7 9QP

A Catalogue record for this book is available from the British Library.

ISBN 1 84538 003 7

Written by Sally Hewitt
Designed by Zeta Jones
Editor Hannah Ray
Picture Researcher Joanne Beardwell

Series Consultant Anne Faundez
Creative Director Louise Morley
Editorial Manager Jean Coppendale

Printed and bound in China

Picture credits

Key: t = top, b = bottom, m = middle, c = centre, l = left, r = right

Heather Angel 16–17; **Butterfly Conservation Picture Library** half title
page, 7, 22-23; **Corbis**/Ralph A Clevenger 12, /Tony Hamblin 9, /Hal Horwitz 4,
/Wolfgang Kaehler 18–19, /Robert Pickett 6, /Jim Sugar 20–21; **Alistair Davis**
14–15; **Ecoscene**/Papilio/Robert Pickett 8, 10, 11.

With thanks to Butterfly Conservation.

Life Cycles
From Caterpillar to Butterfly

Sally Hewitt

QED Publishing

Something is hiding under the nettle leaf.

Lots of tiny butterfly eggs!

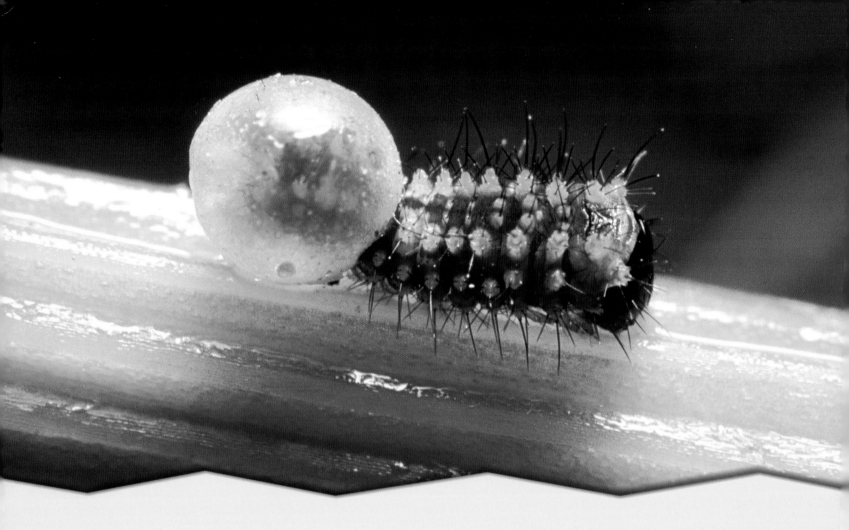

A caterpillar pushes
out of an egg …

and starts munching
on the leaf.

The hungry caterpillar
grows and grows.

It looks too hairy for
these baby birds to eat!

The hairy caterpillar turns into a chrysalis.

Amazing changes happen inside the chrysalis.

12

What is struggling
out of the chrysalis?

A beautiful butterfly!

The butterfly flies off to look for flowers.

It sips sweet juice, called nectar, from the flowers with its long, curly tongue.

15

Two big eyes see
bright colours.

Two long antennae
smell food.

17

The butterfly folds its wings and rests.

It flies off with another butterfly.

The butterfly lays eggs on a nettle leaf.

What will happen to the eggs?

21

What does the caterpillar do when it has pushed out of its egg?

Can you remember what is inside the chrysalis?

Can you describe this butterfly? What colours is it?

Can you remember what the butterfly uses to sip nectar from the flowers?

Carers' and teachers' notes

- Look at the cover together and ask your child to talk about the picture.
- Explain that the picture on the cover gives us an idea of what we will find inside the book.
- Read the title together. Explain that the title tells us what the book is about.
- Talk about the differences between fiction, which is a story, and non-fiction, which gives facts and information.
- Talk about why this a non-fiction book. Does it tell a story? What does it give information about?
- Together, read about the life cycle of a butterfly. Point out that the book ends where it started, with butterfly eggs.
- Draw a circle. Draw eggs, a caterpillar, a chrysalis and a butterfly around the circle to illustrate the concept of a life cycle. Ask your child to run his/her finger around the circle, starting and ending with the eggs.
- Together, talk about all the different stages in the cycle and describe what the eggs, caterpillar, chrysalis and butterfly look like. Talk about their size, shape and colour.
- Explain that butterflies need to find each other to mate and lay eggs, so that the cycle can continue.
- Ask your child to tell you, in his/her own words, the life cycle of a butterfly.
- How does a caterpillar move? Can your child wriggle like a caterpillar?
- Together, draw and paint a pair of butterfly wings.
- Look at pages 22–23 and discuss possible answers to the questions.

24